W9-AGQ-663

WHEAT

A TRUE BOOK

by
Elaine Landau

Children's Press®
A Division of Grolier Publishing
New York London Hong Kong Sydney
Danbury, Connecticut

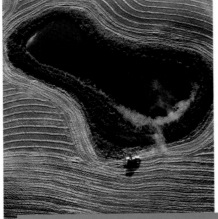

Reading Consultant
Linda Cornwell
*Coordinator of School Quality
and Professional Improvement
Indiana State Teachers
Association*

Author's Dedication
for Derrick Kessler

An aerial view of a North
Dakota wheat harvest

**Visit Children's Press® on the
Internet at:
http://publishing.grolier.com**

Library of Congress Cataloging-in-Publication Data

Landau, Elaine.
 Wheat / Elaine Landau.
  p.   cm. — (A True book)
 Includes bibliographical references (p.   ) and index.
 Summary: Examines the history, cultivation, and uses of wheat.
 ISBN 0-516-21029-7 (lib. bdg.)   0-516-26792-2 (pbk.)
 1. Wheat—Juvenile literature. [1. Wheat.] I. Title. II. Series.
SB191.W5L26   1999
633.1'1—dc21   98-47333
                                                        CIP
                                                        AC

GROLIER
PUBLISHING

Contents

Your sandwich bread and birthday cake are two of many wheat products to enjoy.

What's That You're Eating?

Did you ever eat a sandwich and wonder where the bread came from? What about the noodles in baked macaroni and cheese? Do you think your last birthday cake got its start in a kitchen or bakery?

The main ingredient in all these foods came from the

same plant—wheat. Wheat is actually a type of grass. And although it's used for much more than cereal, it is called a cereal grass or cereal grain.

Wheat grains or kernels are ground into flour. This flour is used to make bread, cake,

Many of these cereals got their start in the same place—a wheat field.

Grain is an important part of a dairy cow's diet.

macaroni, breakfast cereals, pancakes, pastries, crackers, cookies, and many other foods. But wheat products aren't only for humans. Many farm animal feeds and pet foods are also made from wheat.

These women are baking chapatti, a bread popular in India.

Wheat provides an essential food source for countless people around the globe. It's been called the most valuable food crop on the planet. More farm acres throughout the world are used to grow wheat than any other crop.

Grown In The USA

Wheat is the most valuable grain in the United States. Most Americans eat some form of it nearly every day. Wheat is also the country's leading export crop. It is shipped out to many nations throughout the world.

There are many types of wheat. Over thirty different

From planting to loading onto ships, wheat keeps people busy.

kinds exist. Most of the wheats grown in the United States were first brought here by European farm immigrants. Besides their belongings, they carried the handpicked wheat seeds they'd grown in their homelands.

Wheats are sometimes grouped according to when they are grown. The two growing seasons are winter and spring. Winter wheat is planted in the fall and harvested (picked) in the spring or summer. Between 70 and

Young sprouts of winter wheat (left) and spring wheat (right)

80 percent of the wheat produced in the United States is winter wheat. Spring wheat is planted in the spring and harvested in the late summer or early fall.

Wheats grown in the United States are grouped into official classes. These classes are not only determined by the wheat's growing season. The hardness, color, and shape of the wheat's kernels (grains) are also considered. These classes are divided into the following six groups:

Hard Red Winter Wheat— This is the most plentiful type of wheat in the United States. It is grown in the Great Plains states. That's a broad area— extending from the Mississippi

Bales of hard red winter wheat

River west to the Rocky Mountains and from Canada to Mexico. Hard red winter wheat is mostly used to make bread and rolls. Some is also used for sweet goods and all-purpose flour.

Hard Red Spring Wheat— This wheat contains the highest levels of protein. That makes it a good choice for bread making. Hard red spring wheat is grown mainly in Montana, North Dakota, South Dakota, and Minnesota.

Wheat exported to Mexico is used for making tortillas.

Soft Red Winter Wheat—

This wheat is somewhat low in protein. It is mostly cultivated (grown) in areas east of the Mississippi River. Soft red winter wheat is usually used for making desserts such as cakes

Morocco produces some of its own wheat, but much is imported from the United States.

and pastries. It is also often the choice for snack foods.

Durum—Durum has the hardest kernels of any wheat grown in the United States. Most of the durum wheat we use comes from North Dakota. However, like hard red spring wheat, durum is also grown in

Durum wheat gives us pasta products such as macaroni (left). These noodles (right) are made from hard white wheat.

South Dakota, Montana, and Minnesota.

Hard White Wheat—This type of wheat has a mild, sweet taste. It is used in yeast breads, hard rolls, bulgur, tortillas, and Asian style noodles.

Soft White Wheat—Like soft red winter wheat, this

Pancakes, from soft white wheat, become fast food on this street in China.

wheat is largely used for desserts and taste treats. Most soft white winter wheat grown in the United States comes from the Pacific northwest. However, smaller amounts of it are grown in California, Michigan, Wisconsin, and New York.

When Wasn't There Wheat?

Wheat has a long history. It has played an important role in people's lives through the ages. Over 17,000 years ago—before wheat was ever grown as a crop—people gathered wild wheat. They separated the kernels (grains) and ate them raw.

19

Wheat was one of the first crops planted in the area of the Middle East which came to be known as the "cradle of civilization." It was here that the first towns and cities sprang up. Once people settled down to tend their crops, they started communities. Arts, crafts, trading, and governments soon developed as well.

In time, people began using wheat to bake bread. At first, wheat was planted and harvested by hand. Later

An engraving from an Egyptian tomb shows workers during the grain harvest.

Growing wheat along the Nile River has changed little from ancient times.

on, animal-pulled plows were often used. But either way, growing wheat took a good deal of time and energy. It wasn't until the mid-1800s that machines were invented to do

Nineteenth century inventions—a steam thresher (left) and a binding reaper (below)

the work. It used to take a full day to harvest a single acre of wheat by hand. But with modern machinery, the same task is completed in half an hour.

Planting Wheat

Before wheat is planted, the soil must be plowed. A machine called a drill is used to put the wheat seeds into the ground. Pulled by a tractor, it digs narrow rows in the earth and drops the wheat seeds into these. Then it covers the seeds with soil so they can take root.

24

A powerful plow prepares the soil for planting (top). Farmers pour seeds into drilling equipment (bottom).

Combines and
trucks work
efficiently to
harvest miles
of wheat
fields.

For the most part, ripe
wheat is harvested with large
machines called combines. A
combine cuts the wheat stalk.
It also does the threshing—

separating the kernels from the rest of the plant. The threshed grain is stored in a bin on the machine. When the bin fills, the grain is emptied into a truck and taken away. To harvest the wheat speedily, combines are sometimes used around the clock.

After it's picked, trucks deliver the wheat to a large storage area called a country elevator. It's easy to see why they are called elevators.

Moving belts within them lift, or "elevate," the grain to the top of these holding places before dumping it into a bin. The temperature and humidity (level of moisture in the air) at a grain elevator are

carefully controlled. This pre-
vents the crop from spoiling.
Usually the wheat is also
cleaned and dried there.

The wheat's next stop is a
grain exchange or market-
place. There it will be kept in
another large storage area
called a terminal elevator.
Once the wheat is sold, it
begins the last part of its journey. It may be loaded onto a
large ship bound for another
country. Or it may be taken

Grain is transported by freighter (above) or by train (left) from elevators throughout the country.

by truck, railway, or barge to its destination somewhere in the United States.

Most of the wheat will go to a mill to be made into

flour. The remainder will be used to make animal feed and other products. In any case, by the time it reaches you it won't look at all like it did in the field.

An inspector takes notes on grain quality.

Eat Your Wheat

Wheat products appear on our tables at almost every meal. You can make granola for eating as cereal at breakfast or lunch, plain as a snack, or as a dessert topping on ice cream. Here's how:

You will need

- 2 cups of oatmeal
- 1/2 cup each of wheat germ, chocolate or carob chips, raisins, and peanuts
- 1/4 cup each of honey and vegetable oil
- 1 teaspoon vanilla extract.

Crunchy Granola

In a large bowl, mix the oatmeal, peanuts, and wheat germ. In a small bowl, mix the honey, oil, and vanilla. Pour this mixture into the first mixture in the large bowl. Use your hands (after washing them well!) to combine the ingredients. Spread the mix on an oiled baking sheet. Bake at 325 degrees for 15 minutes, then remove the baking sheet from the oven (wear oven mitts, and ask an adult to help). Stir the mix a little, then add the chips and raisins. Bake for another 10 minutes. Cool before munching.

Meanwhile... Back at the Mill

Have you ever had an X-ray taken at a doctor's office or hospital? The same thing often happens to a wheat shipment at a mill. Shipment samples are inspected even before the grain is unloaded. An X-ray can show if any insect pests are present.

A separator has vibrating screens to remove anything that isn't wheat (above). Air blowing through the aspirator removes dust and other tiny particles (right).

The grain is grouped according to how it will be used. Then it's stored in large bins in temperature-controlled areas. Next the wheat is cleaned.

Whole wheat flour is made from the entire kernel. But to make white flour, the miller only uses the kernel's soft, white endosperm. Therefore, the three parts of the kernel must

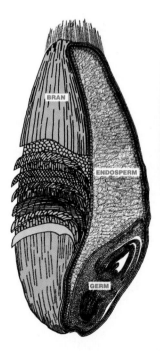

A wheat kernel is made up of three separate parts. These are the endosperm, the bran, and the germ.

BRAN

ENDOSPERM

GERM

be separated. After that the endosperm can be ground into white flour.

A whole wheat kernel contains many valuable vitamins and minerals. But the endosperm used to make white flour lacks some of the important benefits found in other parts of the kernel. However, there's a way to make white flour healthier to eat.

Before it leaves the mill, the flour can be enriched. Enriching

Sacks of flour ready to be sealed and delivered to supermarkets

flour involves adding several B vitamins and iron to it. The flour is passed through a machine that supplies measured amounts of these. In some cases, salt and calcium are put in at this point as well. Enriching white flour makes a widely used product even better.

Better Than Ever

Through the years, scientists have tried to improve wheat in numerous ways. They've worked to solve the most common problems wheat growers face. Among these are poor weather conditions.

Too much rain can cause a wheat crop to rot. Or if the

soil is too wet to plant on time, the wheat may not fully develop. At times, wet weather has caused ripe grain to sprout before it has been picked. This can damage the wheat and reduce its uses. Unfortunately, many plant fungi and viruses that harm the wheat do well in a damp or moist environment.

Some insects are also a threat to wheat. In the worst cases, whole fields of wheat

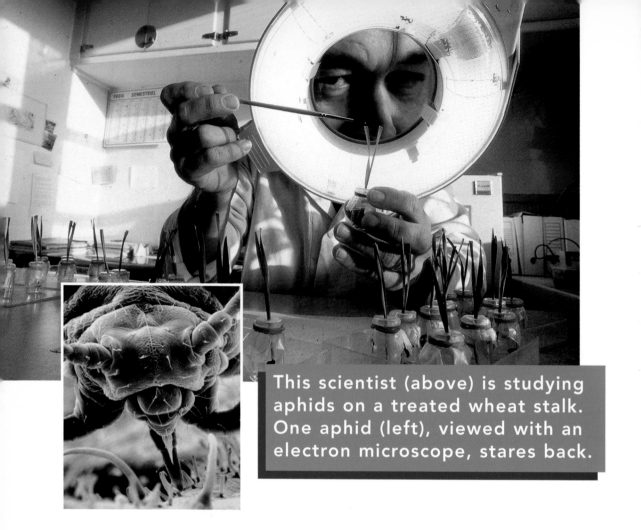

This scientist (above) is studying aphids on a treated wheat stalk. One aphid (left), viewed with an electron microscope, stares back.

have been destroyed by pests such as aphids, sawflies, armyworms, leaf curl mites, and others.

In response, researchers have produced better wheats. They've carefully bred various wheats—only picking the ones with superior qualities. Often these wheats were found to best resist disease and insect attacks. Many are easier to harvest and have shorter growing seasons. Scientists have also developed wheats with sturdier stalks, which hold more grain. This has allowed farmers to harvest a larger crop on the same amount of land.

A good deal of progress has been made. It can take over a decade (ten years) to produce a new variety of wheat. Laboratory and field work can cost hundreds of thousands of dollars as well.

Improved high-yield grains have helped boost the food supply in some of the poorer countries of the world. Such wheats, along with other important crops, may one day play an important role in helping to wipe out world hunger.

A Somali woman feeds cereal to her baby.

To Find Out More

Here are some additional resources to help you learn more about wheat:

Books

Bailey, Donna. **Farmers.** Raintree Steck-Vaughn, 1990.

Curtis, Neil. **How Bread is Made.** Lerner Publications, 1992.

Llewellyn, Claire. **First Look at Growing Food.** Gareth Stevens Children's Books, 1991.

Powell, Jillian. **Bread.** Raintree Steck-Vaughn, 1996.

Robbins, Ken. **Make Me a Peanut Butter Sandwich and a Glass of Milk.** Scholastic, 1992.

💡 Organizations and Online Sites

Kellogg's Planet K
http://www.Kelloggs.com

Home page of the cereal company. Find out how wheat becomes cereal, waffles, and toaster pastries, then visit Cereal City, Nutrition Camp, and the cereal factory.

North Dakota Wheat Commission
http://www.ndwheat.com

Information on hard red spring wheat and durum wheat, plus a wheat cookbook. The Fun for Kids department has a book, "The Story of Wheat," to download (ages 8+, 20 pages).

U.S. Pasta Association
wysiwyg://109/http://www.Ilovepasta.org

Try the featured "Kids Cook" recipe, increase your pasta IQ, and check out the Dietician's Corner for health and nutrition news.

Wheat Foods Council
http://www.wheatfoods.org

Source for tips on how and why to enjoy more grain for better health. Click on topics from bagels to bread machines, couscous to cookies, in the "Grains of Truth" department.

Important Words

barge a flat-bottomed boat used to carry cargo on inland waters

destination the final point to which a journey is headed

essential necessary or highly important

export to send to other countries for sale or trade

harvest to gather or pick a grain

immigrant a person who comes to a new country to settle

ingredient any of the things that are part of a mixture

kernel a grain or seed

plow to turn up the soil's surface for planting

threshing the process of separating the seeds of grain from the rest of a ripened wheat plant

Index

Meet the Author

Elaine Landau worked as a newspaper reporter, an editor, and a youth services librarian before becoming a full-time writer. She has written more than one hundred nonfiction books for young people, including True Books on dinosaurs, animals, countries, and food.

Ms. Landau, who has a bachelor's degree from New York University and a master's degree in library and information science from Pratt Institute, lives in Florida with her husband and son.